CHECK OUT YOUR FRIENDLY NEIGHBORHOOD COMIC SHOP OR BOOKSTORE FOR THESE OTHER FINE BOOKS BY MATT GROENING!

BART SIMPSON™
OUT to LUNCH

TITAN BOOKS

BART SIMPSON: OUT TO LUNCH

Collects Bart Simpson Comics 43, 44, 45, 46, 47

Copyright © 2012 by
Bongo Entertainment, Inc. All rights reserved.

Published in the UK by Titan Books, a division of Titan Publishing Group,
144 Southwark St., London, SE1 0UP, under licence from Bongo Entertainment, Inc.

FIRST EDITION: APRIL 2012

ISBN 9780857687357

2 4 6 8 10 9 7 5 3 1

Publisher: Matt Groening
Creative Director: Nathan Kane
Managing Editor: Terry Delegeane
Director of Operations: Robert Zaugh
Art Director Special Projects: Serban Cristescu
Production Manager: Christopher Ungar
Assistant Art Director: Chia-Hsien Jason Ho
Production/Design: Karen Bates, Nathan Hamill, Art Villanueva
Staff Artist: Mike Rote
Administration: Ruth Waytz, Pete Benson
Editorial Assistant: Max Davison
Legal Guardian: Susan A. Grode
Trade Paperback Concepts and Design: Serban Cristescu
Cover: Kevin Newman and Serban Cristescu

Printed by Quad/Graphics, Inc., Montreal, QC, Canada. 02/15/2011

CONTENTS

BART SIMPSON IN
CLASS KLOWN

JAMES W. BATES
SCRIPT

JEREMY ROBINSON
PENCILS

SHANE GLINES
INKS

NATHAN HAMILL
COLORS

KAREN BATES
LETTERS

BILL MORRISON
EDITOR

7

GOTTA GO! IT'S TIME FOR MY PEDICURE APPOINTMENT. THESE SHOES DO A NUMBER ON MY DOGS.

WAIT? BUT WHICH ONE IS THE CLASS CLOWN?

YOU DECIDE. JUST HAVE HIM SHOW UP AT THAT ADDRESS ON SATURDAY MORNING.

EXIT

LATER THAT DAY...

SO WHICH ONE OF US IS CLASS CLOWN?

UH...

GIVE IT UP, MILHOUSE. THEY ALREADY NAMED ME CLASS CLOWN.

YEAH, BUT KRUSTY UN-NAMED YOU!

I'M SORRY, BOYS, BUT I NEED SOME TIME TO THINK THIS OVER.

AND SO IT BEGINS...

WE LIKE HOW YOU DECORATED YOUR LOCKER!

I HAVE THE SAME MALIBU STACY STICKER ON MINE!

BART PAINTED MY LOCKER...THAT'S NOTHING.

AGH!

THE DOCTOR SAYS I LOST *MY* MARBLES.

LATER IN CLASS...

OPEN YOUR BOOKS TO PAGE THIRTY-ONE.

D'OH!

IS THAT THE BEST YOU CAN DO?

WELL, *PAL* LET'S JUST SAY YOU SHOULD WATCH YOUR BACK!

♪ BART AND ♪ SKINNER SITTIN' ♪ IN A TREE... ♪

HUH?

I ♥ SKINNER

SEE YOU AT LUNCH, *PAL*.

OOOH!

SOON...

STARE MENACINGLY ALL YOU WANT. I'M **NOT** AFRAID OF YOU.

BLAH!

WHOOPS! I FORGOT TO TELL YOU. I DUMPED TWO BOTTLES OF CAYENNE PEPPER SAUCE ON YOUR LUNCH.

I ALSO FORGOT TO MENTION I PUT SOME MUSTARD PACKETS ON YOUR SEAT.

NANA VAN HOUTEN GAVE ME THESE PANTS!

OKAY! I SURRENDER! JUST SIT DOWN AND EAT YOUR LUNCH.

:OOF!:

CRASH!!!

OUTSIDE THE SCHOOL WALLS... THE WAR WAGES ON.

THAT'S IT! BART SIMPSON, *YOU* ARE AN EVIL GENIUS!

I KNOW HOW TO *GET* HIM AND GET HIM *GOOD!*

The Perm Bank

SOMEBODY'S GOTTA HELP ME! MY MOM'S GOT SASQUATCH LEGS!

TELL YOUR POOR MOM TO APPLY THIS CREAM AND RINSE. HER MONKEY LEGS WILL BE AS SMOOTH AS A BABY'S BOTTOM IN NO TIME.

THANKS.

Hairy Notter

BUILDER'S BARN

I BET I CAN FIND WHAT I NEED HERE.

THIS CAULK IS GUARANTEED TO BOND FOR TWENTY-YEARS.

I'LL TAKE IT!

SORRY TO BOTHER YOU, BUT I CHUGGED A MEGA-SQUISHEE, AND I DON'T THINK I CAN HOLD IT UNTIL I GET HOME!

I BET MILHOUSE WOULD NEVER THINK OF PRANKING ME AT HOME.

THIS'LL SHUT BART'S BIG MOUTH!

HAIR TODAY, GONE TOMORROW!

THE AFTERMATH...

ENOUGH! AS FAR AS I'M CONCERNED, YOU ARE BOTH CLOWNS!

HUH?

MWUH?

FIRST GO SEE THE SCHOOL NURSE AND THEN GO TO THIS ADDRESS TOMORROW MORNING. KRUSTY CAN HAVE THE BOTH OF YOU.

THE NEXT MORNING...

BART, WE WERE REALLY AT EACH OTHER'S THROATS...

DRIVE THRU

KRUSTYBURGER

...FOR THIS!?!

UNBELIEVABLE!

HEY! LESS HUB-BUB AND MORE SCRUB-SCRUB! I WANT THAT BOWL CLEAN ENOUGH TO EAT OUT OF!

IF WE ONLY KNEW THIS IS WHAT KRUSTY MEANT BY "WORK" FOR HIM!

CHEER UP, MILHOUSE. WE'LL GET THE LAST LAUGH!

STINK-ULEAR

THAT PLACE REEKS!

I'M CALLING THE DEPARTMENT OF HEALTH!

YUCK!

THE END

15

♪ I MIGHT FALL FROM A TALL BUILDING,
I MIGHT ROLL A BRAND NEW CAR.
'CAUSE I'M MAGGIE'S BABYSITTER
WHEN I'M NOT RUNNIN' A BAR. ♪

I NEVER SPENT MUCH TIME IN SCHOOL
BUT I TAUGHT MAGGIE PLENTY.
SHE'S NEVER EMBARRASSED 'BOUT
WHAT I GOT TO SAY.
HEY-HEY.

SORRY, I'M LATE, MAGS. THE NAUGHTY 'DEO STORE WAS HAVIN' A LABOR DAY SALE AND I LOST TRACK OF THE TIME.

♪ I'LL TELL HER ABOUT THE CORLEONES,
OR HOW SONNY GOT WHACKED.
'CAUSE TO HER "THE GODFATHER"
IS JUST A GAME WE PLAY.
HEY-HEY. ♪

OH, NO. WHY DID THE TOLL COLLECTOR SUDDENLY DUCK DOWN INSIDE HIS BOOTH?

♪ I MIGHT JUMP AN OPEN DRAWBRIDGE,
OR TARZAN FROM A VINE.
'CAUSE I'M A LONELY BARTENDER WHO SOLVES
MYSTERIES AND CRIMES. ♪

SAY, MAGS... HOW IS THIS *SOLVIN'* A CRIME AGAIN?

THE MAGGIE & MOE MYSTERIES!
IN COLOR!

TONIGHT'S EPISODE:

NAPTIME FOR MURDER!

TONY DIGEROLAMO
SCRIPT

JAMES LLOYD
PENCILS

ANDREW PEPOY
INKS

NATHAN HAMILL
COLORS

KAREN BATES
LETTERS

BILL MORRISON
EDITOR

I APPRECIATE YOU COMING BY ON SUCH SHORT NOTICE, MOE. MAGGIE ALWAYS HAS A GREAT TIME WITH YOU.

YEAH, IT'S NO PROBLEM, MIDGE. YOU GET TO THE HOSPITAL THERE. HEY, BY THE WAY...

...HOW DID YA GET ALL GLUED TO YOUR KIDS, HOMER?

IT'S A COMMON ACCIDENT. HAPPENS TO PEOPLE ALL THE TIME. THEY JUST GET GLUED TO THEIR KIDS.

YEAH, ESPECIALLY WHEN YOU LEAVE THE SUPER GLUE ON THE COUCH WITH THE CAP OFF.

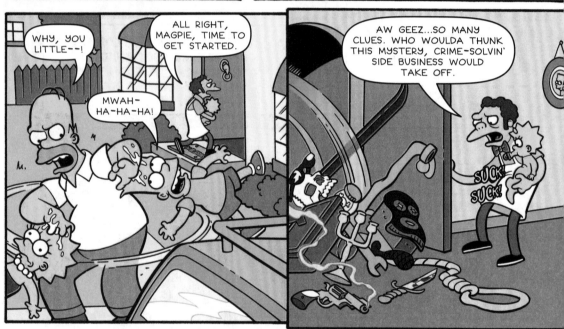

WHY, YOU LITTLE--!

ALL RIGHT, MAGPIE, TIME TO GET STARTED.

MWAH-HA-HA-HA!

AW GEEZ...SO MANY CLUES. WHO WOULDA THUNK THIS MYSTERY, CRIME-SOLVIN' SIDE BUSINESS WOULD TAKE OFF.

SUCK! SUCK!

I JUST DON'T GET IT, MAGS. HOW COULD THE WAITER STAB THE DUKE FROM ACROSS THE ROOM?

SUCK! SUCK!

RIING!

WHAT? YA MEAN HE THREW THE CROSSBOW AT 'IM?

HELLO? SIMPSON RESIDENCE.

YEAH, HI...THIS IS CHIEF WIGGUM. I'M LOOKIN' FOR THE BABY AND THE BARTENDER WHO SOLVE CRIMES.

THIS IS THE BARTENDER THAT DOES THAT THING THAT YA SAID RIGHT THERE.

18

GOOD. WE GOT A CRIME SCENE WHERE THE VICTIM WAS STABBED, POISONED, AND THEN HANGED. WE CAN'T FIGURE OUT WHAT HAPPENED. WOULD YOU MIND COMING BY?

GOODBYE, CRUEL WORLD! HELP YOURSELF TO THE DONUTS

OH...AND HE LEFT BEHIND FREE DONUTS, SO COULD YOU PICK UP SOME COFFEE ON THE WAY OVER?

LOOKS LIKE WE GOT ANOTHER CASE THERE, MAGGIE. WHEN IT RAINS, IT POURS, HUH?

SUCK! SUCK!

OH, RIGHT, I FORGOT. WE'RE ALSO SUPPOSED TA BE LOOKIN' FOR THAT HANS MOLEMAN, GUY.

ALL RIGHT, AS SOON AS WE SOLVE THIS CASE, WE'LL GET RIGHT ON IT.

ONE HOUR LATER...

SUCK! SUCK!

BOY, THAT WAS A TIRIN' MYSTERY THERE. WHO WOULDA GUESSED THE VICTIM WAS MURDERED BY THE VERY MOBSTER HE PLACED BETS WITH?

RIIING!

OH, FOR THE LOVE OF POUND CAKE!

19

SIMPSON RESIDENCE.

HI, EVERYBODY!

YEAH, HI THERE, DR. NICK. WHAT IS IT?

I'VE GOT A REAL SCOOBY-DOO MYSTERY ON MY HANDS. AND THEN I THOUGHT, WHY NOT CALL THE BABY AND THE BARTENDER?

I WAS DOING AN AUTOPSY, BUT SUDDENLY MY PATIENT SPRUNG BACK TO LIFE. HOW DID THAT HAPPEN?

HELLO? I'M NOT DEAD, YOU IMBECILE! WORST TRIPLE BYPASS OPERATION EVER!

ALL RIGHT, ALL RIGHT, WE'LL BE RIGHT OVER.

THE MYSTERIES JUST WON'T STOP COMIN'! AND I'LL BETCHA NEXT WEEK WE'LL BE SITTIN' AROUND ON OUR MAGNIFYIN' GLASSES!

SUCK! SUCK!

OH, YEAH, **MOLEMAN**. I WON'T FORGET THIS TIME.

AN HOUR LATER...

:PHEW!: ANOTHER MYSTERY SOLVED! WHO WOULDA THOUGHT DR. NICK'S NURSE WAS ACTUALLY OUT TO KILL COMIC BOOK GUY BY MIXING UP HIS CHART.

SUCK! SUCK! SUCK! SUCK!

RIIING!

I DON'T BELIEVE THIS!

SUCK! SUCK!

THE SIMPSONS... WHAT?

I'M LOOKING FOR A GUY. LAST NAME "MIPANTS", FIRST INITIALS "I.P."

HOLD ON.

MAGGIE, THIS GUY'S LOOKIN' FOR SOMEONE NAMED I.P. MIPANTS. DO YOU KNOW I.P. MIPANTS?

AH, HA-HA-HA! HA-HA!

LISTEN, WE GOT ANOTHER CALL. WE'LL HAVE TO SOLVE YOUR MYSTERY LATER.

MOE? IT'S BARNEY. I NEED YOU TO SOLVE A PUZZLE FOR ME...

CLICK CLICK

WHAT IS IT, BARN? I'M KINDA SWAMPED HERE.

UM...THIS GUY IN A CRAZY MASK CHAINED ME TO A STOVE THAT'S LEAKING GAS, AND NOW I GOTTA FIGURE OUT HOW TO OPEN THE LOCK OR SAW MY FOOT OFF TO ESCAPE. THIS IS THE WORST GAME SHOW EVER!

ALL RIGHT. WE'LL BE RIGHT THERE.

ONE HOUR LATER...

IT'S A GOOD THING WE DIDN'T HAVE TO SAW OFF BARNEY'S FOOT TO SET HIM FREE. THAT MYSTERY WASN'T EVEN A CHALLENGE...BUT AT LEAST WE FOUND HANS MOLEMAN.

AW, LOOKS LIKE YOU'RE ALL TUCKERED OUT FROM A DAY OF SLEUTHIN'. THESE OTHER MYSTERIES ARE GONNA HAVE TA WAIT. SORRY, COLONEL MUSTARD, MAYBE NEXT TIME.

SUCK

WE'RE BACK! HOW'S MY ANGEL?

ASLEEP. SHE HAD A LOOOONG DAY.

MAGGIE ALWAYS SLEEPS GOOD AFTER YOU BABYSIT, MOE.

YEAH, MAGGIE AND ME KEEP OURSELVES PRETTY BUSY PLAYIN' AND WHATNOT WHEN I'M OVER HERE.

SO LONG, MIDGE.

HOLY HANNAH! I COMPLETELY FORGOT TO DIFFUSE THE BOMB STRAPPED TO HANS MOLEMAN!

HELLO? BABY AND MAN? ARE YOU COMING BACK? HELLO?

TICK TICK TICK

THE END

BART SIMPSON in SAXOPHONY!

MATT GROENING

WAKE-UP... WAKE-UP...WAKE-UP...WAKE-UP!

BAKE WHAT?

UH?

C'MON, DAYLIGHT'S A BURNIN'!

WHAT'S THE MATTER, BART?

SUN...BAD!

IT'S SATURDAY THE 14TH! IT'S MT. SPLASHMORE DAY!

I'VE BEEN WAITING FOREVER FOR THIS! YOU DIDN'T FORGET, DID YOU?

ER...NO.

THIS YEAR THEY'VE ADDED REAL STINGING JELLYFISH TO THE KIDDIE POOL!

IT'S SATURDAY... SATURDAYS ARE FOR SLEEP.

I'VE GOT SOME BAD NEWS FOR YOU.

JAMES W. BATES
SCRIPT

MARCOS ASPREC
PENCILS

PHYLLIS NOVIN
INKS

NATHAN HAMMILL
COLORS

KAREN BATES
COLORS

BILL MORRISON
EDITOR

PAWN SHOP

WHY DO YOU WANT A NEW BACKLESS DRESS?

I SAID I WANT TO GET *BACK* AT *LISA* FOR GETTING A *NEW DRESS!*

OH.

WHY WOULD YOU TRADE SOME OF YOUR PRIMO COMIC BOOK STASH FOR THIS CD AND THAT DUMPY OLD SAXOPHONE?

IT'S STEP ONE OF MY DEVIOUS PLAN.

A DENTED SAXOPHONE, A CD, AND OLD MAN CLOTHES? I'M NOT GETTING THIS PLAN.

OH, YE SIDEKICK OF LITTLE FAITH! ALL WILL BE EXPLAINED WHEN WE GET TO YOUR HOUSE.

MY HOUSE?

DID I MENTION I NEED TO BORROW YOUR MP3 PLAYER?

THE BLEEDING GUMS MURPHY CD IS ALMOST FINISHED DOWNLOADING.

I'VE ALMOST GOT THE SPEAKER RIGGED INSIDE THE SAX.

BLEEDING GUMS MURPHY

HONEY, WHAT YOU JUST PLAYED SOUNDED GREAT.

HUH? IT WASN'T ME. I JUST GOT HOME.

BUT?

THAT DROP DEAD JAZZ WAS HAMMERED DOWN BY *ME!*

YOU? NO WAY.

YEAH, PROVE IT.

NO PROBLEMO. GET A SHOVEL AND DIG *THIS*.

WOW!

I *DO* DIG IT!

WHAA--?!

AT THE NEXT SUMMER RECITAL REHEARSAL...

LISA, WHY DIDN'T YOU TELL ME YOUR BROTHER HAD SUCH MUSICAL ABILITY?

I'M JUST AS SURPRISED AS YOU, MR. LARGO.

CLAP!

CLAP!

CLAP!

EVEN THOUGH I HAVE COME TO LOATHE JAZZ MUSIC, YOUR TONE AND TECHNIQUE ARE QUITE IMPRESSIVE.

WOULD YOU CONSIDER JOINING OUR SCHOOL BAND? I'LL MAKE YOU OUR *NEW* FIRST CHAIR SAXOPHONE...

BUT...*I'M* FIRST CHAIR!

BUT *YOU'VE* NEVER PLAYED BEFORE! *I'VE* PRACTICED EVERY DAY FOR YEARS!

LITTLE SISTER, IT'S *JAZZ*. YOU GOTTA LEARN TO GO WITH THE FLOW.

THIS ISN'T RIGHT!

I'M SORRY, LISA, BUT YOUR BROTHER HAS A GIFT.

THANKS FOR THE PROPS, BUT *NO THANKS*. FIRST *CHAIR* HAS GOT NO *FLAIR*!

YOU DON'T WANT FIRST CHAIR?

I PLAY *SOLO* OR IT'S A *NO GO*. DIG?

WHATEVER YOU WANT AS LONG AS YOU PLAY AT THE RECITAL

THIS TOWN HASN'T HEARD A SAX MAN WITH SO MUCH PRESENCE SINCE BLEEDING GUMS MURPHY PERFORMED LIVE AT THE AZTEC THEATRE IN 1972...

HUH? AZTEC...'72...?

...THOUGH I STATE CATEGORICALLY THAT MY PREVIOUS ENJOYMENT OF "JAZZ MUSIC" WAS BUT A MERE YOUTHFUL INDISCRETION.

WE'LL STOP THE SHOW AND LET YOU "RIFF" BY YOURSELF!

SNAP!

GOOD CALL!

BLEEDING GUMS MURPHY LIVE AT THE AZTEC IN '72. *THAT'S* WHERE I'VE HEARD THOSE SONGS BEFORE!

THIS HAS TO BE ONE OF BART'S SCHEMES! HE WON'T CONFESS, BUT I KNOW SOMEONE WHO WILL...

LATER...

HE MADE ME DO IT!

GRRR.

IT'S MY PATHETIC LOT IN LIFE TO BE BART'S PAWN!

SO YOU LOADED THE SONGS ONTO AN MP3 PLAYER AND BART'S PLAYING THE MUSIC STRAIGHT FROM THAT?

HE HID SOME SPEAKERS IN THE SAXOPHONE.

WILL YOU EVER FORGIVE ME?

I'LL FORGIVE YOU *IF* YOU'LL HELP ME GET BACK AT BART.

TELL HIM YOU NEED TO RECHARGE THE MP3 PLAYER'S BATTERY BEFORE THE RECITAL.

OKAY.

AND THEN WE'LL *CHANGE BART'S TUNE!*

I THINK *THIS ONE* WILL DO THE TRICK!

EH, I DON'T KNOW WHAT *THAT'S* DOING IN MY ROOM.

DON'T WORRY. MAKE SURE THESE SONGS ARE ON THAT MP3 PLAYER FOR BART'S PERFORMANCE AT THE RECITAL, AND NO ONE EVER NEEDS TO KNOW WHERE THEY CAME FROM.

THE RECITAL...

SPRINGFIELD ELEMENTARY ORCHESTRA
♪♪ FEATURING THE SIZZLING SAX OF ♪♪
BART SIMPSON

BART, ARE YOU READY TO SHOW OUR AUDIENCE SOMETHING SPECIAL?

EVERYTHING IS EVERYTHING, BABY!

CLICK!

WE'RE THE HAPPY LITTLE ELVES! HAPPY-HAPPY-HAPPY!...

UH-OH!

WE'RE THE HAPPY LITTLE ELVES! HAPPY-HAPPY-HAPPY!...

EARL KRESS
SCRIPT

MARCOS ASPREC
PENCILS

PATRICK OWSLEY
INKS

NATHAN HAMILL
COLORS

KAREN BATES
LETTERS

BILL MORRISON
EDITOR

SO, YOU LIKE PICKING ON *OLD GUYS,* EH?

IT'S KIND OF A HOBBY.

WHOA!

WE'LL JUST SEE ABOUT *THAT!*

HEY, CHIEF, IF YOU WERE *DARTH VADER,* YOU COULDA PICKED HIM UP *WITHOUT* TOUCHING HIM. NOW YOU'VE GOT *JUVIE COOTIES!*

AT THE SPRINGFIELD COURTHOUSE...

I SENTENCE YOU TO *100 HOURS* OF *COMMUNITY SERVICE!*

PIECE OF CAKE!

MAKE THAT *200* HOURS!

BIG WHOOP!

SNAP!

200 HOURS AT THE *SPRINGFIELD RETIREMENT CASTLE!*

EEP.

OKAY, PUNK, HERE'S YOUR *HOME* FOR THE NEXT *FIVE WEEKS!*

WHAT MAKES YOU THINK I WON'T *LEAVE* THE MINUTE YOU DRIVE AWAY?

KA-SHLIK!

WHAT MAKES *YOU* THINK I'M *LEAVING?*

I CAN STILL *RUN FASTER* THAN YOU!

PLOOK!

PROBABLY. BUT CAN YOU OUTRUN TWO GERMAN SHEPHERDS?

HEEL, MAULER! *HEEL*, WIGGUM'S LITTLE HELPER!

SOON...

YOUNG PERSON!

LET ME TELL YOU ABOUT *WORLD WAR II!*

YOU LOOK JUST LIKE *MY GRAND-DAUGHTER!*

WANNA SEE MY *HERNIA?* I CAN MAKE IT POP IN AND OUT.

BREAK IT UP, AND GET BACK TO YOUR ROOMS!

YOU CAN GIVE MR. SIMPSON HIS *SPONGE BATH* NOW!

THERE ARE MY TEETH!

BACK IN LINE, OLD MAN.

HOW DO THESE OLD DUDES EVER SEE WHAT'S *OUTSIDE* THIS PLACE?

WAKE UP, EVERYONE! IT'S TIME FOR YOUR NAPS...*IN YOUR ROOMS!*

HEY, CUTIE, HOW'S ABOUT CUTTING MY TOENAILS?

FORGET THE SCISSORS. HERE, YOU'RE GOING TO NEED AN INDUSTRIAL FILE.

PUT ON THE NIGHTLY NEWS!

WHERE ARE MY SLIPPERS?

WHEN I WAS 17, I WAS THE BELLE OF THE BALL AND MY DANCE CARD WAS ALWAYS FULL.

THERE ARE CRITTERS GROWING IN MY BEARD.

YOUR HAIR IS SO LONG AND SOFT JUST LIKE MY GRAND-DAUGHTER'S.

MAKE SURE YOU WASH BETWEEN MY TOES.

ANYBODY SEEN MY WOODEN LEG?

OH, LET ME PINCH THAT CHEEK OF YOURS ONE MORE TIME.

BART SIMPSON in

DOG GONE HOLLYWOOD!

STRIP MALL TALENT AGENCY

NOW LOOKING FOR NEW ACTS

STRIP MALL TALENT AGENCY

(NO, WE DON'T REPRESENT STRIPPERS)

CHI DRA

ALL YO BUFFE

I THINK THAT MY DOG COULD BE REALLY BIG STAR FOR YOUR AGENCY, MISTER.

OH, YEAH? WHAT CAN HE DO?

HE CAN DANCE LIKE CRAZY!

VARIETY

THIS I'VE GOTTA SEE.

BLINK!

MATT GROENING

SOOOO... WHEN DOES HE DANCE?

SKRITCH! SKRITCH!

CHRIS YAMBAR
SCRIPT

PETE McDONNELL
PENCILS

MARK & STEPHANIE HEIKE
INKS

ART VILLANUEVA
COLORS

KAREN BATES
LETTERS

BILL MORRISON
EDITOR

THE END

8:15

HAPPY HAPPY HAPPY HAPPY!!!!

8:15!?! I'M A HALF HOUR LATE!

THAT'S WHAT I GET FOR RELYING ON THOSE HAPPY LITTLE ELVES TO WAKE ME UP!

I'M SORRY, LISA, BUT I THOUGHT YOU WANTED TO SLEEP IN!

BUT DON'T WORRY, HONEY... YOUR BREAKFAST WAS DELICIOUS!

WHOOPS... GOTTA GO!

HEY, LIS, YOU SNOOZE... YOU LOSE!

QUIET, YOU!

GRUMBLE!

HONEY, I FORGOT TO TELL YOU THAT MY CAR'S STILL BEING REPAIRED!

AND DAD ALREADY LEFT...

HEY, OTTO, WAIT UP!

UHHH...IS THAT THE ONLY SEAT LEFT ON THE BUS?

YEAH, BUT DON'T WORRY, LISA...I'M SAVING IT FOR YOU!

SNURKLE!

LISTEN, LISA! MY NOSE MISSED YOU SO MUCH, IT'S BEEN CRYING!

GREAT...

I'LL GET YOU ALL TO SPRINGFIELD ELEMENTARY SCHOOL...EVEN IF IT KILLS US!

BUT OTTO, THIS IS THE SEVENTH TIME YOU'VE DRIVEN AROUND THE SCHOOL WITHOUT STOPPING!

RRRRRRRIIIIinnng!!

...JANEY POWELL...PRESENT... RALPH WIGGUM... PRESENT...

...LISA SIMPSON! TARDY!

BUT...BUT ...BUT...

WOULD EVERY-ONE PLEASE PASS THEIR **HOMEWORK** FORWARD?

"HOMEWORK?" I CAN'T **BELIEVE** IT! I LEFT IT IN MY **BACKPACK**... ON THE **BUS**! STUPID!

OH, **GREAT**. NOW I'M **RIPPING** MYSELF TO **PIECES**!

MAYBE I'VE GOT SOME **SEWING NEEDLES** AND IN MY LOCKER...

OH, CLE-**VER**.

EL BARTO WAS here
-LISA-
Lisa has a big butt!

HEY, YOU'RE "**IT**" FOR **DODGEBALL** THIS WEEK, LISA

WHAT?

WHAP!

WHAP!

WHAP!

≥SIGH!≤ I'M GOING TO BE **BLACK** AND **BLUE** FOR A WEEK...

ONE OF THE BEST-KNOWN DINOSAURS WAS THE **BRONTOSAURUS**...

UH, MISS HOOVER, DON'T YOU MEAN, "**APATOSAURUS**"? "**BRONTOSAURUS**" ACTUALLY REFERS TO A SPECIES THAT'S NOW CONSIDERED **NON-EXISTENT**!

ONE MORE RUDE INTERRUPTION LIKE **THAT**, YOUNG LADY, AND **YOU'LL** BE THE ONE WHO'S CONSIDERED "NON-EXISTENT!"

TEE-HEE!

KERSPLAT!

OHHHHH...

WE APPRECIATE YOU COMING IN FOR THIS **MEETING**, MR. AND MRS. SIMPSON...

PRINCIPAL

...BECAUSE THIS IS AN **UNUSUAL** SITUATION REGARDING YOUR DAUGHTER LISA!

YES, LISA IS USUALLY THE **IDEAL STUDENT**, BUT TODAY, SHE'S BEEN **ACTING OUT** SOMETHING AWFUL, ESPECIALLY WITH HER **FOUL-MOUTHED OUTBURST** DURING LUNCH!

WELL, THAT SORT OF **MISBEHAVIOR** CERTAINLY ISN'T **TYPICAL** OF LISA, I CAN ASSURE YOU!

≷YAWN!≷ SPEAKING OF **MOUTHS**, YOU GOT ANY **SALTY SNACKS** AROUND HERE?

HOMER, YOU JUST WENT THROUGH A **KRUSTYBURGER DRIVE-IN** ON THE WAY OVER HERE!

YEAH, BUT THE SMELL OF *CHALK* MAKES ME *HUNGRY* ALL OVER AGAIN!

OH, *PLEASE*, MOM AND DAD...AREN'T I IN *ENOUGH* TROUBLE *ALREADY*? CAN'T YOU JUST *PRETEND* TO BE *NORMAL* UNTIL THIS ORDEAL IS *OVER*?

FORTUNATELY, PRINCIPAL SKINNER AND I HAVE COME UP WITH A VERY APPROPRIATE WAY TO *CURE* LISA'S RECENT CASE OF *POTTY MOUTH*.

YES, I THINK THAT WE'VE DEVISED A *PUNISHMENT* THAT TRULY FITS THE *CRIME!*

FOR THE NEXT *TWO WEEKS*, LISA IS GOING TO SPEND ALL OF HER *FREE TIME* HELPING OUT IN THE *CAFETERIA* WITH *LUNCHLADY DORIS!*

LUNCHLADY DORIS?!? BUT SHE'S *ALWAYS* SWEARING!

THAT'S EXACTLY THE *POINT*, LISA!

SPENDING ALL THAT TIME WITH A *FOUL MOUTH* LIKE DORIS OUGHT TO QUICKLY PUT YOU ON THE PATH TO *VERBAL CLEANLINESS!*

AND SO, LISA'S DAY OF **KITCHEN INDOCTRINATION** FINALLY COMES...

WELL, HERE WE ARE IN THE **STOMACH** OF SPRINGFIELD ELEMENTARY SCHOOL... THE **CAFETERIA!**

AND **THIS**, LISA, IS YOUR NEW **MENTOR**...LUNCH-LADY DORIS!

UNHHH... IT'S A **DISTINCT PLEASURE** TO, UH, BE **COLLABORATING** WITH YOU, MS. DORIS...

YEAH, IT'S A @$%#&☆! **KICK IN THE HEAD** TO MEETCHA, KID...

WELL, ЄHEH HEH!Ϛ, I GUESS I'LL JUST LEAVE THE TWO OF YOU **ALONE** SO YOU CAN GET **ACQUAINTED** WITH EACH OTHER BETTER...

S-SO, UH, WHO'S YOUR FAVORITE **CHEF**, LUNCHLADY DORIS? BOBBY FLAY? EMERIL LAGASSE? WOLFGANG PUCK?

KRUSTY THE @$%#&☆! **CLOWN**.

OH GREAT. SHE'S GOT THE **SAME TASTE** IN FOOD AS **DAD!**

NOW I GOTTA **QUESTION** FOR **YOU**, BRIGHT-EYES... HOW MANY @$%#&☆! **POTATOES** CAN YOU PEEL IN AN **HOUR?**

UH, **ONE** AND A **HALF**...?

WELL, YOU'D @$%#&☆! BETTER LEARN HOW TO **BEAT** THAT @$%#&☆! **RECORD** PRETTY V@$%#&☆! **FAST** IF YOU WANT TO GET ALONG WITH **ME!**

Y-YES, LUNCHLADY DORIS!

AND SO, LISA'S **FOOD SERVICE SERVITUDE** UNDER THE SALTY-TONGUED LUNCHLADY DORIS GRINDS ON, ONE GRUELING DAY AT A TIME...

LISA, THE **GELATIN CUPS** NEED SOME **FRESHENING UP!** BASTE 'EM WITH SOME @$%#&☆! **COD LIVER OIL!** IT REALLY MAKES 'EM **GLISTEN!**

R-RIGHT AWAY, LUNCHLADY DORIS!

LISA, THE **MEAT LOAF** IS TOO **LOOSE!** POUR IN A FEW @$%#&☆! POUNDS OF **SAWDUST** TO **THICKEN** IT UP!

Y-YOU'RE THE **BOSS**, LUNCHLADY DORIS!

LISA, THE STUDENTS ARE SAYIN' THAT OUR **FISH STICKS** AIN'T FRESH! SO **WRAP** 'EM IN **TODAY'S** @$%#&☆! **NEWSPAPER. THAT** OUGHTTA SATISFY THE BRATS!

FISH TACKLE

R-RIGHT **AWAY**, LUNCHLADY DORIS!

LISA, WE GOTTA COMPLAINT FROM THE **HEALTH INSPECTOR** ABOUT THESE @$%#&☆! **ENCHILADAS!** CHANGE THEIR @$%#&☆! **LABEL** TO "**LASAGNA!**"

W-WHATEVER YOU **SAY**, LUNCHLADY DORIS!

LISA, ADD MORE **ORANGE POSTER PAINT** TO THE @$%#&☆! **THOUSAND ISLAND DRESSING!**

Y-YOU'VE **GOT IT**, LUNCHLADY DORIS!

LISA, THE *EXTERMINATOR* IS COMIN' BY LATER! TELL 'IM TO GIVE OUR @$%#&☆! *SALADS* AN EXTRA *SCHPRITZ!*

I-I'M *ON* IT, LUNCHLADY DORIS!

LISA, TAKE THIS AEROSOL CAN OF *FURNITURE POLISH* AND GIVE THE @$%#&☆! *MERINGUE PIES* A TOUCH-UP!

A-AT YOUR *SERVICE,* LUNCHLADY DORIS!

SHAKE! SHAKE!

LISA, *RE-MARK* THESE @$%#&☆! *MOLDY CHEESE PIZZAS* AS "*WOLFGANG DORIS'* PESTO @$%#&☆! *PIZZAS!*"

W-WHEN YOU'RE *RIGHT,* YOU'RE *RIGHT,* LUNCHLADY DORIS!

WOLFGANG DORIS' 'PESTO PIZZAS'

LISA, MOVE UP THE *EXPIRATION DATES* ON ALL OF THESE @$%#&☆! *MILK CARTONS* BY *THREE WEEKS!*

ABSOLUTELY, LUNCHLADY DORIS!

MILK MILK MILK MILK

LISA, *ROTATE* TH' @$%#&☆! *POTATOES* SO THEIR *EYES* AIN'T *STARIN'* AT ME!

LISA, *ALIGN* ALL TH' @$%#&☆! *POTS* AND *PANS* TOWARD *MAGNETIC NORTH!*

LISA, *ARRANGE* AND *FILE* ALL THE @$%#&☆! *LUNCH MEAT* FROM "*A*" TO "*Z*"!

UH-OH! THIS *DOESN'T* LOOK *GOOD!*

MILK MILK MILK

LISA...*LISA!* ⦂COUGH⦂ I DON'T FEEL SO-- ⦂ERRRK!⦂

OH, @$%#&☆!...*

T*HUD!!*

DON'T WORRY, LITTLE GIRL. LUNCHLADY DORIS JUST CUSSSED HERSELF CLEAN INTO A *TIZZY!*

@$%#&☆! ORDERLIES...

IF *THAT'S* A "*TIZZY*," I'D SURE HATE TO SEE WHAT A *NERVOUS BREAKDOWN* LOOKS LIKE!

YEAH, SHE'S A *TOUGH* OLD BIRD! SHE'LL GET *BETTER* BACK AT THE *SPRINGFIELD HOME FOR THE EXTREMELY NERVOUS* FASTER THAN YOU CAN SAY "@$%#&☆!"

OH, PLEASE DON'T *FRET*, LISA! ⦂HEH HEH!⦂ WHY, THIS IS PRACTICALLY *STANDARD OPERATING PROCEDURE* FOR LUNCHLADY DORIS!

HAVE NO *FEAR*, PRINCIPAL SKINNER, I'LL MANAGE! I'VE ONLY GOT *ONE DAY LEFT* TO SERVE MY *PUNISHMENT!*

MAKE IT A *GOOD* ONE, LISA! AFTER ALL, *TOMORROW* IS SPRINGFIELD ELEMENTARY SCHOOL'S ANNUAL *FACULTY LUNCHEON!*

OH, YES, THE ANNUAL *FACULTY LUNCHEON! RIIIIIGHT!* ⦂GULP!⦂

WELL, I FOR ONE CAN'T *WAIT* TO SEE WHAT YOU'VE GOT ⦂HEH HEH!⦂ *COOKED UP* FOR US, LISA!

YEAH, I CAN'T *WAIT*, EITHER!

WAIT A MINUTE! WHAT AM I *SAYING*?

OF *COURSE* I'M CAPABLE OF FIXING ALL THE *FOOD* FOR THE FACULTY LUNCHEON! I'VE ALREADY SPENT *NINE DAYS* LEARNING THE *INS* AND THE *OUTS* OF THIS KITCHEN! SO...

...*LET'S GET READY TO COOK!*

LISA MAY BE *INSPIRED*, BUT TYPICALLY, SHE'S DETERMINED TO DO THINGS HER *OWN WAY*...

THE ART OF THE ORGANIC MEAL: STRAIGHT DIRT ON RAW FOODS

THIS IS GOING TO BE A *MEAL* WITH *APPEAL*!

PEEL! PEEL!

...*DEFINITELY* A *CUT* ABOVE THE *OTHERS*!

SLICE! SLICE!

HMMM...

LET'S SEE THEM *TURN UP* THEIR NOSES AT *THIS!*

MASH MASH

THE FACULTY LUNCHEON'S BOUND TO BE A *STIRRING* EXPERIENCE!

AHHHH...

A FEAST FOR THE EYES: HOW TO PRESENT FINE CUISINE

THERE'S NOTHING LIKE A *WELL-BALANCED* MEAL!

AFTER TOILING THROUGH THE *NIGHT* AND INTO THE NEXT *DAY*, THE PREPARATION OF LISA'S UNIQUE FEAST IS *FINALLY* COMPLETED!

¦GASP! GASP!¦

IT'S *FINISHED*... AND JUST IN *TIME!*

WELL, I TRIED MY *BEST*, SO HERE *GOES*...

SOUP'S ON, EVERYBODY! NOT TO MENTION DELICIOUS *SALADS,* A VARIETY OF *MAIN COURSES, SIDE DISHES, DESSERTS,* AND *BEVERAGES!*

OOOOOH!

WELL, I MUST SAY THAT IT CERTAINLY LOOKS LIKE LISA DID *HERSELF*...AND LUNCHLADY DORIS...*PROUD!*

YES, EVERYTHING LOOKS SO *YUMMY!*

AND SO, HAVING SUCCESSFULLY SERVED HER *FULL SENTENCE,* YOUNG LISA SIMPSON *EXITS* THE CAFETERIA ON A *NOTE* OF *TRIUMPH!*

LUNCHLADY DORIS, THIS ONE'S FOR *YOU!*

"Y'KNOW, I CAN'T HELP BUT *WONDER* HOW THE TEACHERS ARE *ENJOYING* MY *FOOD*..."

:GHACKK!: BY THE LESSON PLAN OF SAMUEL GOMPERS, WHAT THE @$%#&☆! IS THIS @$%#&☆!?

:SPUTTER!: THIS IS THE *WORST* @$%#&☆! I'VE EVER *TASTED!*

...:UECCHH!: AND PEOPLE CLAIM THAT MY *HAGGIS* IS @$%#&☆! VILE!

OMIGOSH! IT'S @$%#&☆! *AWFUL!*

:ULP!: I GUESS MY *CUISINE* WAS A BIT TOO *SOPHISTICATED* FOR THE FACULTY'S *TASTES!* WELL, YOU CAN'T SAY I DIDN'T *TRY!*

BUT WHO KNEW THEY WERE SO *FOUL-MOUTHED?*

SOMEBODY REALLY OUGHT TO *WASH OUT* THEIR *MOUTHS* WITH *ORGANIC SOAP!*

SPRINGF ELEME

THE @$%#&☆! END!

bartspace.com

Welcome to **bartspace,** where you can create a computer profile, so people can get to know the real YOU.

But BE WARNED! The webmaster (that's me!) reserves the right to edit, alter, or completely fabricate your personal profile as he sees fit, man!

MATT GROENING

Grade Grubber

About: Will do anything for an extra + after his A. No amount of kowtowing, toadying, or bootlicking is too small.

Habitats: Study hall, the library, bookstores or anyplace containing boring books and knowledge.

Interests: Doing homework, science, polishing apples, and clapping erasers.

Greatest Ambition: To gain approval of authority figures.

"A SLIGHT MISCALCULATION"

"REDACTED BY REQUEST"

Milk Money Bandit

About: Has taken the art of bullying to new levels.

Pet peeve: When his victims bleed on him.

Habitats: Alley behind the Kwik-E-Mart, under the bleachers, the streets, and wherever one or more nerds gather.

Interests: Getting you to do his homework, making you hit yourself, vests, and Andy Williams.

Greatest Ambition: To prove his physical superiority so he doesn't have to reveal his intellectual inferiority.

"HI-HO CANDY...AWAY!"

"FORGETTING MY WALLET"

TONY DIGEROLAMO
SCRIPT

BILL GALVAN
PENCILS

MIKE DECARLO
INKS

ART VILLANUEVA
COLORS

KAREN BATES
LETTERS

BILL MORRISON
EDITOR

Paste Taster

About: Doomed to repeat the 2nd grade at least twice. Voted most likely to swallow school supplies.

Habitats: School supply cabinets, the therapist's office, and the "special" bus.

Interests: Picking his nose, wiping his nose on things, replacing what he picked out of his nose with something else, and making booger sculptures.

Greatest Ambition: To perpetuate the saying, "Ignorance is bliss."

"HUGGING THE CAMERA"

"ME AND THE LEPRECHAUN"

Sidekick

About: Always looking for crumbs of cool that fall off of other kids. Wants to be accepted…will settle for pity.

Habitats: At your side, upside down in a toilet bowl, waiting on your doorstep.

Interests: Groveling, begging, following, and failing to live up to expectations.

Greatest Ambition: To one day gain self-esteem.

"FETCH ME A DREAM"

"MY BFF"

About: A black hole for cool. He is like a free buffet for bullies. Everything from his thick glasses to his pocket protector screams "Nerd!"

Habitats: Science labs, planetariums, museums, and hanging from a flagpole by his underwear.

"BIRTHDAY SURPRISE"

Bully Magnet

Interests: Talking in an annoying voice, creating socially awkward moments, and correcting grammar.

Greatest Ambition: To invent a "bully invisibility cloak."

"THE WORST THONG EVER"

About: Nothing but trouble. She is impossibly cute and totally evil.

Habitats: Boarding school, the back of a motorcycle, Daddy's blind spot.

"DOING THE LAUNDRY IS SO BORING!"

Interests: Looking innocent, planning mayhem, wrapping boys around her little finger, and throwing tantrums.

Daddy's Little Angel

Greatest Ambition: To get everything she wants.

"WHO ARE THEY FIGHTING OVER? OH, RIGHT. ME!"

bartspace.com

Fat Foreign Kid

About: Unable to hide his accent or lack of knowledge about the local culture. He is at the mercy of bullies, nerds…well, just about everyone.

Habitats: Kitchens, food storage, near vending machines.

Interests: Eating chocolate, German tuba polka music, and breathing heavy.

Greatest Ambition: To survive long enough to return to his country of origin.

 bartspace.com

"MEIN CAMERA IS STICKY!"

"MMM! DAS LUNCH!"

Nerdgrrl Puncher

About: Will one day be made fun of by prettier girls and has to get her licks in before looks start to matter.

Habitats: Lunchrooms, classrooms, the gym, or wherever she can terrorize the weak.

Interests: Terrorizing the weak, biting off the heads of Malibu Stacy dolls, stuffing nerds into lockers, and ponies.

Greatest Ambition: To find a man she can bully for the rest of her life.

 **bartspace.com**

"FRANCINE SMASH!"

"CRUSHING ON JIMBO"

Gruesome 2some

About: Think they're clever because they can trade places with each other.

Habitats: Malls, hallways, lunchrooms, or wherever they can show off their twin powers.

Interests: Dressing like each other, making up special twin languages, correcting people who mistake them for one another, and betraying non-twin people.

Greatest Ambition: To keep people from realizing that because they are both identical, neither one of them is unique.

"SHERRI...OR IS IT?"

"TERRI...OR IS IT?"

Smelly Sis

About: She is a beacon of knowledge and strength in a world of ignorance and darkness. And if you can't see her in the dark, you can totally smell her.

Habitats: Her room, the library, school, Dorkville, and most recently spotted in the vicinity of Nerdtown.

Hobbies: Playing the saxophone, saving the environment, thinking globally, and acting locally. I want a pony! I want a pony! I want a pony!

Greatest Ambition: Duh! I'm a stupid girl!

"THE DALAI LAMA IS MUCH TALLER IN PERSON."

"MRS. VAN HOUTEN-TO-BE"

Sub-par Sibling

About: Attention seeker and showoff extraordinaire. As far as he's concerned, there's no such thing as bad publicity.

Habitats: School assemblies, playgrounds (or wherever he can make a spectacle of himself), detention, and the principal's office.

Interests: Shooting milk through his nose, imitating the sounds of bodily functions, dropping his pants, making jokes at the teacher's expense, and learning to read at a 1st grade level.

Greatest Ambition: To annoy his sister, who is infinitely smarter than him in every way...
HELLO, BART!

bartspace.com

"NO SUCH THING AS BAD PUBLICITY...HUH?"

"BART MEETS HIS MATCH"

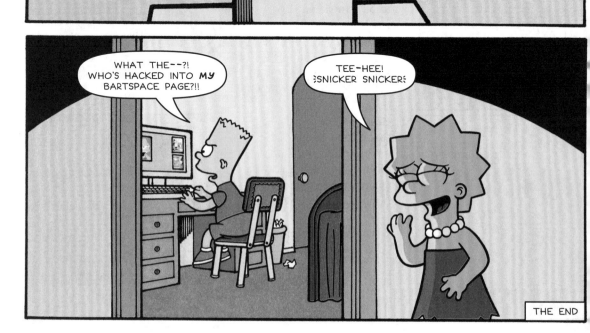

WHAT THE--?! WHO'S HACKED INTO *MY* BARTSPACE PAGE?!!

TEE-HEE! ≀SNICKER SNICKER≀

THE END

MAGGIE SIMPSON IN
MAGGIE'S MELTDOWN

HOMER, ACCORDING TO TODAY'S NEWSPAPER, IT'S "TAKE YOUR DAUGHTER TO WORK DAY" TODAY!

AND SINCE YOU'VE GOT *TWO* DAUGHTERS...

WHAT A *RIP!* YOU MEAN, LISA GETS THE DAY *OFF,* MAGGIE GETS SPRUNG *OUT* OF THE HOUSE...BUT *I* GET STUCK WITH SPRINGFIELD ELEMENTARY SCHOOL'S *SAME OL' SAME OL'?*

Springfield Shopper

TAKE YOUR DAUGHTER TO WORK DAY

MATT GROENING

SCOTT SHAW!	CARLOS VALENTI	MIKE ROTE	NATHAN HAMILL	KAREN BATES	BILL MORRISON
SCRIPT	PENCILS	INKS	COLORS	LETTERS	EDITOR

GEE, DAD, I'M REALLY, REALLY *INTERESTED* IN SEEING THE *SPRINGFIELD NUCLEAR POWER PLANT!*

THEN *SEE* IT YOU *SHALL,* LISA! AND YOU, *TOO,* LI'L MAGGIE!

...EVEN IF YOU HAVE TO *SEE* IT THROUGH SPECIAL *LEAD GLASS GOGGLES!* DON'T WANNA GET ANY *RADIATION BURNS* ON THE OL' *PEEPERS,* DO WE?

WELL, HERE WE *ARE*, GIRLS...THE PLACE THAT PUTS THE *BACON* ON OUR TABLE...THE *SPRINGFIELD NUCLEAR POWER PLANT!*

MMMM... *NUCLEAR BACON!*

HEY, WHERE DO YOU THINK *YOU'RE* GOING, LISA?

OH, DIDN'T I *TELL YOU*, DAD?

NUCLEAR POWER EQUALS SLOW PAINFUL DEATH

I CAME ALONG WITH YOU SO I COULD *PROTEST* THE POWER PLANT'S *EXISTENCE!*

:SIGH!: BUT LISA, THIS ISN'T *"TAKE YOUR DO-GOODER DAUGHTER TO WORK SO SHE CAN GET THE PLACE SHUT DOWN AND YOU LOSE YOUR JOB"* DAY!

OH WELL, AT LEAST *MAGGIE* WANTS TO HANG OUT WITH ME...*DON'T* YOU, MAGGIE?

SOON, IN HOMER'S CONTROL ROOM *"OFFICE"*...

OKAY, LI'L MAGGIE...HERE'S A *PICTURE* OF YOUR *FAVORITE PERSON* TO KEEP YOU *SMILING*... AND TO HELP KEEP ME *GOOFING OFF!*

AND WHAT IS *THIS ONE'S* NAME, SMITHERS?

UM, *HOMER SIMPSON*, SIR.

AH, YES...*SIMPKINS!* HAPPY *"ALLOW YOUR VILE OFFSPRING TO INTERRUPT PRODUCTION"* DAY! AND WHO IS *THIS*? SHE CERTAINLY LOOKS *FAMILIAR*...

UH-OH! WHAT IF MR. BURNS *RECOGNIZES* MAGGIE? SHE ONCE NEARLY *SHOT HIM TO DEATH!**

ER...THIS IS MY DAUGHTER, *MAGGIE*, MR. BURNS! BUT YOU'VE NEVER *MET* HER BEFORE! AND I CAN *ASSURE* YOU, SHE HARDLY *EVER* CARRIES ANY *FIREARMS!*

*AS SEEN IN THE HISTORIC TWO-PART "SIMPSONS" EPISODE, "WHO SHOT MR. BURNS?"--EDITOR BILL

WELL, HELLO, MEGAN... MY, MY, I'LL WAGER THAT YOU GROW UP INTO A REAL *PISTOL* OF A YOUNG LADY. HEH, HEH!

...BLAH... BLAH...BLADDY-BLADDY BLAH BLAH-BLAH-BLAH...

CAN WE *LEAVE* YET?

I THINK IT WOULD BE *BEST*, SIR! WE'VE GOT OVER *FOUR HUNDRED MORE* OF THESE OBLIGATORY CORPORATE *"HOWDY-DOS"* TO MAKE BY THE END OF THIS WORK SHIFT!

WELL, UH, *TOODLE-OO*, SIMPKINS AND MEGAN. SEE YOU THIS TIME *NEXT* YEAR!

≔PHEW!≔ *SAFE* UNTIL *NEXT* YEAR!

HEY, CHECK IT *OUT*, GUYS...A DOZEN FRESH *LARD LAD* DONUTS--THE *DELUXE* ASSORTMENT, TOO!

WOW! THAT MEANS TWO WITH *SPRINKLES*...

...AND A BUTTERMILK *CRULLER* ≔GLAAAH!≔

Y'KNOW, THE CRULLER IS THE *ROYALTY* OF FRIED PASTRIES!

I CONTEND THAT THE *MAPLE LOG* IS THE UNDISPUTED *RULER* OF DONUT LAND!

WHO *CARES?* GIMME THAT *CRULLER!*

NO *WAY*, HOMER! THAT CRULLER IS *MINE!*

SAYS *YOU*, MISTER *"I'M-YOUR-BEST-FRIEND-UNTIL-FRIED-PASTRY-ROYALTY-COMES-ALONG"!*

HEY...FRIED PASTRY *IS* MY BEST FRIEND!

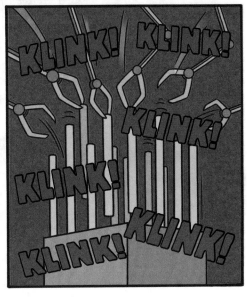

SLIDE!

SLIDE!

SWOOP!

PLOP!

MEANWHILE, BACK IN *SECTOR 7-G*...

WELL, I HOPE YOU'RE PROUD OF YOURSELVES. WE CAN'T EVEN *MOVE*!

YEAH, BUT THINK OF THE *TWISTER* CONTESTS WE COULD *WIN*!

THE ONLY *TWISTED* THING *I* WANNA WIN IS THAT *CRULLER*!

C'MERE, YOU SWEET LITTLE *SPIRAL* OF *DOUGH*!

SQUIRT!

AND SPEAKING OF "*DOUGH*"...

...D'OH!

SMOOTH *MOVE*, HOMER! THAT *CRULLER* LANDED IN EXACTLY THE *WRONG* PLACE.

SPLORK!

AHOOOGAH!
AHOOOGAH!

WE'RE *DOOMED! DOOMED,* I SAY!

AHOOOGAH!
AHOOOGAH!

AHOOOGAH!

AH**OOO**GAH!

IT'S THE *END* OF THE *WORLD* AS WE *KNOW* IT!

AHOOOGAH!

AHOOOGAH!

BACTERIAL STERILIZATION CHAMBER

AHOOOGAH!

AHOOOGAH!

AW, AND POOR OL' TEMP EMPLOYEE *GIL* NEVER GOT AROUND TO *WATCHING* ALL THE *EXTRA FEATURES* ON HIS *DVDS!*

AHOOOGAH!

AHOOOGAH!

IN CASE OF PASTRY-RELATED DISASTER, PULL LEVER!

IN CASE OF PASTRY-RELATED DISASTER, PULL LEVER!

YANK!

WOW! THAT *SUDDEN QUIET* IS ALMOST *DEAFENING!*

SHHHHH!

HEY, ALL THE *MELTDOWN* ALARMS HAVE *STOPPED!*

AND ALL OF THE *METER READINGS* HAVE *DROPPED* BACK TO *NORMAL!*

YEAH, BUT THAT'S *ONE* CRULLER I'LL *NEVER* TASTE! ⋚SIGH!⋚

AW, *C'MON,* HOMER, GIVE IT A *REST!*

YEAH, CRULLERS ARE *OVERRATED!* NOW MAPLE LOGS, THAT'S *ANOTHER STORY!*

YEAH, THEY'RE *SWEET,* ALL RIGHT...

...BUT *NOT* AS SWEET AS MY LITTLE *MAGGIE-WAGGIE!*

SMOOCH!

YOU SPENT THE *WHOLE DAY* IN YOUR LITTLE BASKET HERE AND YOU NEVER *FUSSED* EVEN *ONCE!*

LATER THAT AFTERNOON...

SO, DID YOU *LEARN* ANYTHING *NEW* TODAY, LISA?

YES, I LEARNED THAT I'M GOING TO HAVE TO RESORT TO MORE *SUBVERSIVE TACTICS* IF I EVER HOPE TO *EFFECT* ANY *SIGNIFICANT CHANGES* IN OUR SOCIETY!

THAT'S *NICE,* HONEY...

AND THEN, *MUCH* LATER THAT NIGHT...

HOMER? AM I *IMAGINING* THINGS, OR IS MAGGIE *GLOWING?*

UH-OH!

THE END!

BART SIMPSON IN

BART'S NAME IS MUD!

≹ZZZZZ!≹

SPSSSS

RRRRING!

YAY!

RECESS!

YEAH, YEAH! YOU KNOW WHERE THE PLAYGROUND IS.

WHAT DO YOU THINK, MILHOUSE? IS IT A DAY FOR DODGEBALL?

OH, BART. CAN WE PLAY KICKBALL? IT RESULTS IN A LOT LESS BRUISING.

EITHER ONE, DUDE. I'M HAPPY AS LONG AS WE GET OUTTA THAT STUFFY CLASSROOM.

JAMES W. BATES
SCRIPT

MARCOS ASPREC
PENCILS

MIKE DECARLO
INKS

NATHAN KANE
COLORS

KAREN BATES
LETTERS

BILL MORRISON
EDITOR

WOO-HOO!

WOULD SOMEONE BE SO KIND AS TO ASSIST ME?

SIX...SEVEN ...EIGHT!

YOU SPUN TEN TIMES!

⁝BLECCH!⁝

WELCOME TO THE SPRINGFIELD MUD SPA. DO YOU HAVE AN APPOINTMENT?

UH...NO.

SORRY, SIR. MUD BATHS ARE BY APPOINTMENT ONLY.

HAW, HAW!

MARTIN, WHAT ARE YOU DOING?

I'M TAKING ADVANTAGE OF THE LOOSENED SOIL TO SEARCH FOR ARTIFACTS!

I'M FINDING FASCINATING ITEMS. WOULD YOU LIKE TO JOIN MY ARCHAEOLOGICAL DIG?

NO, BUT SOME MUD HAS...UH...MADE ITS WAY...OOF...INTO MY UNDERPANTS!

EWW!

NEAT STATUE!

THANKS!

I CALL IT, "LAME DUDE KISSING A MONKEY'S BUTT!"

WHAT IS GOING ON HERE?

WHAT'S GOING ON? ONLY THE BEST RECESS *EVER!*

THEY'RE ROLLING AROUND IN THE FILTH LIKE LITTLE PIGGIES.

HA! AT LEAST PIGS WILL ONE DAY BECOME BACON. ODDS ARE AGAINST ANYONE IN THIS GROUP MAKING A CONTRIBUTION TO SOCIETY.

HEY, BART! HERE'S MUD IN YOUR EYE!

OOF!

GOTCHA!

SPLAT!

MUD FIGHT!

THIS IS LIKE SOME PLAYGROUND VARIATION OF "ALL QUIET ON THE WESTERN FRONT."

GIVE IT A REST, LISA. WE'RE NOT IN THE CLASSROOM.

MY NOSE MAKES ITS OWN MUD.

HMM... SUPERINTENDENT CHALMERS WON'T LET ME USE TEAR GAS ANY-MORE, SO HOW AM I SUPPOSED TO RESTORE ORDER TO THIS CHAOS?

WHY BOTHER? I SAY WE LET ALL THE LITTLE "ANGELS" GET DIRTY FACES.

BUT IT'S ANARCHY.

OH, SEYMOUR! STOP BEING SUCH A STICK IN THE MUD! LET THEM PLAY, AND WE CAN CHILL OUT IN THE TEACHER'S LOUNGE AND WATCH SOAPS.

IF MY WATCH IS RIGHT, "IT NEVER ENDS" STARTS IN JUST A COUPLE OF MINUTES!

LISA SIMPSON
IN
COOL RULES!

HEY, WHERE ARE YOU GOING WITH YOUR *MALIBU STACY* DOLLS...AND FASHION ACCESSORIES?

HAVEN'T YOU HEARD?

SHERRI AND *TERRI* HAVE STARTED A *MALIBU STACY* CLUB!

MATT GROENING

OH, THIS IS SO EXCITING!

AFTER *PONIES* AND *ECOLOGY,* MALIBU STACY IS MY *FAVORITE THING* IN THE *WHOLE WORLD!*

EARL KRESS
SCRIPT

ALBERTO SANTIAGO
PENCILS

MIKE ROTE
INKS

ART VILLANUEVA
COLORS

KAREN BATES
LETTERS

BILL MORRISON
EDITOR

SHERRI! TERRI! I'D LIKE TO JOIN YOUR CLUB!

OH, TOO BAD!

YEAH, IT'S *GIRLS ONLY*!

BUT *I'M* A *GIRL*!

OH, YEAH... I *GUESS* YOU ARE. WE MEANT *COOL* GIRLS ONLY!

ARE YOU IMPLYING I'M *NOT* COOL?

I'LL *PROVE* TO THEM I'M COOL!

HA! HA! HA! HA!

SHORTLY...

MY "*PAREE STACY*" OUTFIT WILL SHOW THEM HOW COOL I AM!

IT *SICKENS* ME THAT THEY THINK *BART* IS COOL, BUT *I* CAN PLAY ALONG!

OH...*ICK!* THERE ARE *DEAD REPTILES* IN BART'S DRESSER...AND *OTHER* UNIDENTIFIABLE OBJECTS!

COOL?

FOOL!

I'VE JUST *GOT* TO SEE WHAT THEY'RE DOING IN THERE!

MR. SMITHERS!!

I THOUGHT THIS WAS *GIRL'S ONLY!* *I'M* MORE OF A GIRL THAN *HE* IS!

MAYBE, BUT HE'S STILL *COOLER* THAN YOU!

DO YOU KNOW WHO'S *REALLY* COOL?

YES, WE KNOW. MR. BURNS.

WELL, YES, BUT I MEANT *VERA SLANG*, THE *DESIGNER* OF STACY'S ENSEMBLES.

SO, THEY'RE IMPRESSED BY *FASHION DESIGNERS*! WELL, *I'M* GOING TO DESIGN THE *BUTTONS* OUT OF AN OUTFIT!

SOON...

FASHION DESIGNING FOR NERDS

TAP!
TAP!
TAP!

Cutting Fabric For Nerds

SNIP!
SNIP!

LOOK AT YOU GO, LISA...SEWING THAT LITTLE OUTFIT. I DON'T CARE *WHAT* THOSE GIRLS SAY, *YOU'RE* COOL!

MOM! IT'S *NOT COOL* IF YOUR *MOTHER* THINKS YOU'RE COOL!

AYE, ROBOT!

I ALWAYS *DREAMED* I'D LIVE TO SEE THIS DAY, BUT NOW THAT IT'S HERE, IT'S BECOME MY *WORST NIGHTMARE!*

ERIC ROGERS
SCRIPT

JOHN COSTANZA
PENCILS

PHYLLIS NOVIN
INKS

ART VILLANUEVA
COLORS

KAREN BATES
LETTERS

BILL MORRISON
EDITOR

GREAT CAESAR SALAD, *WHAT'S HAPPENING?!?*

THE KIDS ARE ALL SICK BECAUSE SOMEONE LEFT THIS BUCKET OF SAWDUST ON THE COUNTER. I THOUGHT IT WAS *OATMEAL!*

SAWDUST? THAT BUCKET COULD BELONG TO *ONLY ONE MAN...*

...GROUNDSKEEPER WILLIE! HOW COULD YOU LEAVE YOUR SAWDUST BUCKET IN THE KITCHEN? HALF THE CHILDREN IN THE SCHOOL ARE ILL BECAUSE OF *YOUR* MISTAKE!

THE CHILDREN GETTIN' SICK OFF THE SAME THING THAT SOAKS UP THEIR HEAVIN'S? THAT'S MORE THAN A WEE BIT *IRONIC*.

I'M SORRY, WILLIE, BUT I HAVE TO *LET YOU GO*.

WHAT? BUT *WHY*?!?

SIMPLE ECONOMICS: YOU TAKE THE PROBABILITY OF HUMAN ERROR PLUS YOUR SALARY DIVIDED BY YOUR UNION-ENFORCED 8-HOUR WORK DAY MULTIPLIED BY TECHNOLOGICAL ADVANCEMENT, CARRY THE TWO, SUBTRACT PI...IT'S ALL SO *OBVIOUS*!

WHAT IS?!

ROBOT MAKES ME TALK LIKE A *GIRL*!

YOU'RE BEING REPLACED.

GENERAL CUSTO

GENERAL CUSTO IS AN ALL-ENCOMPASSING CUSTODIAL UNIT THAT CAN DO EVERY JOB YOU CAN IN *ONE-FIFTH* THE TIME AND DOESN'T QUIT UNTIL *YOU TURN IT OFF*!

PLUS, IT HAS A HARD DRIVE THAT UPDATES ATTENDANCE DAILY AND DETECTS FORGED SIGNATURES ON REPORT CARDS ⸘GA-HOYVEN‼⸘

YOU'RE A GENIUS, FRINK! WE'LL *TAKE IT*!

BUT YE CAN'T *FIRE* ME! WHAT'S WILLIE GONNA DO FOR A JOB? WHERE AM I GONNA LIVE??

I'M SORRY, WILLIE, BUT GENERAL CUSTO HAS ALREADY PROCESSED YOUR PAPERWORK.

ACH! CURSE ITS *NINJA-LIKE* STEALTH!

IT'S NEVER EASY TO BE FIRED, WILLIE, BUT I'M SURE YOU'LL FIND AN EVEN BETTER JOB!

YEAH, LIKE CLEANING *HIGH SCHOOLS!*

THANK YOU FOR YER KIND WISHES, LITTLE ONES.

NOW BEFORE I GO, I'D LIKE TO GIVE YOU SOMETHING TO REMEMBER OL' WILLIE BY. FOR BART, MY TRUSTY CAN OF SPRAY PAINT REMOVER WHICH REMOVES PAINT FROM ANY SURFACE WITH A SINGLE SPRITZ!

COOL! NOW I CAN *REVISE* MY WORK!

AND FOR WEE LISA, MY *MOST PRIZED POSSESSION.* WEAR THIS AND YOU WILL HARNESS A *VERY SPECIAL POWER!*

NAY, BUT THE STONE WILL CHANGE COLORS TO TELL YOU WHAT *MOOD* YER IN!

WILL I TURN *INVISIBLE*??

SO LONG, CHILDREN! I CANNAE PUT ME FINGER ON IT, BUT SOMETHING SAYS IT'S *TIME TO GO!*

IT SU

90

AHH...NOTHING LIKE A GOOD BOOK AT LUNCHTIME-- HEY!

GRAB!

THAT'S MY BOOK! I HAVEN'T FINISHED READING IT YET!

SORRY, LISA, BUT GENERAL CUSTO IS IN CHARGE OF COLLECTING ALL LIBRARY BOOKS THE MOMENT THEY'RE OVERDUE.

BUT I'M NOT DONE EATING YET!

YANK!

HUH?

HEY, THAT'S NOT TRASH! THOSE ARE OUR MARBLES!

TOSS!

THAT ROBOT IS ONLY SUPPOSED TO DO WILLIE'S OLD JOB, NOT MAKE LIFE MISERABLE FOR EVERY KID IN SCHOOL!

WE'VE GOTTA FIGURE OUT A WAY TO GET RID OF THAT ROLLING BOX OF BOLTS AND FAST!

A FEW DAYS LATER...

OKAY WHO GETS THE **KRUSTY KANGAROO NUGGETS?**

BOOMERANG 'EM THIS WAY, MATE!

DAD, **STOP THE CAR!**

:*GASP*: DID THEY FORGET THE DIPPING SAUCES? THE FRENCH-DIPPED FRENCH FRIES? THE SWEET-AND-SOUR PORK CHOWDER?!

IT'S **WILLIE!**

I DIDN'T ORDER ANY WILLIE...

GROUNDSKEEPER WILLIE, WHAT ARE YOU DOING OUT HERE?

I'M TRYIN' TO RAISE ENOUGH MONEY FOR A PLANE TICKET BACK TO ME HOME.

WHAT HAPPENED TO FINDING A NEW JOB?

I CAN'T GET ANOTHER JOB BECAUSE I ONLY HAVE EXPERIENCE AS A GROUNDSKEEPER! I GUESS I'M NOT MEANT TO DO ANYTHING ELSE.

AND WITH NO MONEY, I HAVE TO LIVE IN THIS WEE BOX IN AN ALLEY WITH THE **ONLY PERSON** THAT WILL TAKE ME IN!

HEY, **ROOMIE,** GUITAR JOE'S CALLING! HE WANTS TO KNOW IF WE WANT TO **HOP TRAINS** WITH HIM AND THE BOYS TONIGHT?

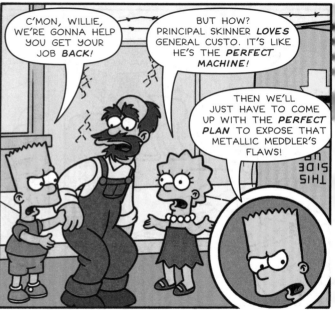

C'MON, WILLIE, WE'RE GONNA HELP YOU GET YOUR JOB **BACK!**

BUT HOW? PRINCIPAL SKINNER **LOVES** GENERAL CUSTO. IT'S LIKE HE'S THE **PERFECT MACHINE!**

THEN WE'LL JUST HAVE TO COME UP WITH THE **PERFECT PLAN** TO EXPOSE THAT METALLIC MEDDLER'S FLAWS!

THE NEXT DAY...

WE ALL KNOW GENERAL CUSTO HAS TAKEN THE *FUN* OUT OF SCHOOL, SO LET'S HELP WILLIE GET HIS JOB BACK!

IF GENERAL CUSTO DOES HIS JOB *EVEN WORSE* THAN WILLIE EVER DID, PRINCIPAL SKINNER WILL SURELY BEG WILLIE TO RETURN!

BUT HOW IS *THAT* GOING TO HAPPEN?

MARTIN HAS COME UP WITH AN IDEA THAT'S *SURE* TO WORK!

EVERYONE WILL DROP A BAG LIKE THIS ONE ON THE GROUND WHEN GENERAL CUSTO IS NEARBY...

...AND WHEN CUSTO SEES THE SUPPOSED BAG OF TRASH, HE'LL RUSH OVER, SCOOP IT UP, AND DROP IT INSIDE OF HIS INTERNAL TRASH COMPACTOR!

BUT WHAT'S *INSIDE* THE BAGS?

MAGNETS! ONCE THEY'RE INSIDE GENERAL CUSTO, THE MAGNETS' REVERSAL FIELD CHARGE WILL CROSSWIRE HIS HARD-DRIVE, WHICH WILL COMMAND HIM TO DO HIS JOB IN THE *EXACT OPPOSITE WAY!*

EVERYBODY GRAB SOME, AND LET'S *TAKE OUR SCHOOL BACK!*

MAGNETS MAKE MY *FILLINGS* WIGGLE!

GROUNDS-KEEPER WILLIE, YOU *SAVED* US!

BOY, WASN'T IT *"CONVENIENT"* THAT YOU SHOWED UP WHEN YOU DID!

BUT YOU *TOLD* ME THE ROBOT WOULD BE ACTING UP BECAUSE OF YOUR PLAN WITH THE MAGN--

OH, WILLIE, YOU'RE THE GREATEST! WE'D RATHER *SHOW YOU* HOW WE FEEL THAN TALK ABOUT IT!

WELL, SEYMOUR, THIS PLACE IS A MESS. HOW IN THE WORLD ARE YOU GOING TO CLEAN IT UP?

GROUNDS-KEEPER WILLIE CAN DO IT!

AND HE CAN START RIGHT NOW!

PERFECT! *HE'S RE-HIRED!*

CHILDREN, THANK YOU SO MUCH FOR HELPING ME GET MY JOB BACK!

NO SWEAT. BUT WHAT ARE YOU GOING TO DO WITH GENERAL CUSTO NOW THAT HE'S PRETTY MUCH USELESS?

I WON'T THROW HIM TO THE CURB *JUST YET*...

THAT AFTERNOON...

...I'VE NEEDED A *NEW RIDING LAWNMOWER* FOR AGES!

AND MY MOOD RING SAYS ALL'S WELL THAT ENDS WELL!

WHHEENNN!

THE END

98

HOW MISS HOOVER GOT HER GROOVE BACK

OKAY, CLASS. THIS IS A POP QUIZ. TAKE OUT YOUR NUMBER TWO PENCILS AND YOU KNOW THE REST.

OH, BOY! POP QUIZ TUESDAY! I LIKE THIS ALMOST AS MUCH AS STANDARDIZED TEST THURSDAY!

HMM. THIS TEST SEEMS UNINSPIRED.

POP QUIZ #104

1) WHEN DID COLUMBUS DISCOVER AMERICA?

2) WHAT YEAR DID COLUMBUS COME TO AMERICA?

3) WHEN COLUMBUS CAME TO AMERICA, WHAT YEAR WAS IT?

4) WHAT HAPPENED IN 1492?

5) COLUMBUS DISCOVERED AMERICA IN 1492: T OR

MISS HOOVER, I CAN'T HELP BUT NOTICE THAT THE QUIZ IS JUST A VARIATION ON A THEME AND THAT OVERALL, YOU SEEM REALLY...WELL, WORLD-WEARY. IS EVERYTHING ALL RIGHT?

LISA, I APPRECIATE YOUR CONCERN, BUT THE LOVE I HAVE FOR TEACHING IS AS STRONG AS THE DAY I STARTED THIS JOB TWO YEARS AGO.

TONY DIGEROLAMO
SCRIPT

PHIL ORTIZ
PENCILS

SHANE GLINES
INKS

NATHAN HAMILL
COLORS

KAREN BATES
LETTERS

BILL MORRISON
EDITOR

TWO YEARS AGO...

GOOD MORNING, CLASS! I'M YOUR NEW TEACHER, MISS HOOVER! NOW, I HAVE A LOT OF ACTIVITIES PLANNED WHERE YOU'LL GET TO LEARN AND HAVE FUN! THIS IS GOING TO BE AN EXCITING YEAR FOR ALL OF US, I THINK. NOW WHO WOULD LIKE TO--

UH, EXCUSE ME.

YOUNG MAN, YOU'RE SUPPOSED TO BE PAYING ATTENTION, NOT DRAWING PICTURES.

BUT I'M DRAWING A PICTURE OF YOU, MISS COOTIE.

MY NAME IS MISS HOOVER.

SORRY, MISS COOTIE.

IT'S PRONOUNCED, "MISS HOOVER".

MISS COOTIE?

MISS HOOVER!

MISS DOODIE?

I AM NOT "MISS DOODIE"!

THE TEACHER SAID, "DOODIE"! AHAHAHA!

HAW HAW!

HA! HA!

HA! HA! HA!

Y'SEE?

THAT STORY ILLUSTRATED THE EXACT **OPPOSITE**! PART OF YOU DIED INSIDE WHEN FACED WITH DIFFICULTY, BUT IF YOU COULD JUST REKINDLE THE SPARK THAT LED YOU TO TEACH...

YEAH, MAYBE...

BUT IN THE MEAN-TIME...WHILE I COLLECT YOUR TESTS, CLASS, LET ME INTRODUCE OUR GUEST SPEAKER. THIS IS STEVE. I MET HIM AT THE SUPERMARKET.

HEY, KIDS! WHO HERE LIKES PUTTING THINGS IN BAGS? NOW IMAGINE THEY **PAY** YOU FOR IT! PRETTY SWEET, HUH?

LATER...

MOM, MY TEACHER, MISS HOOVER, HAS LOST THE WILL TO TEACH. WHAT AM I GOING TO DO? WITHOUT AN INSTRUCTOR THAT'S ENGAGED IN MY EDUCATION, I COULD END UP GOING TO A SECOND OR THIRD TIER COLLEGE!

WELL, WHAT MAKES YOU SAY SHE'S LOST HER WILL TO TEACH?

SHE LET **RALPH** GRADE OUR POP QUIZZES! HE GAVE EVERYBODY A "J+" AND THEN SENT US HOME FOR **PIE**!

POP QUIZ #104

1) _____ ?
2) _____ ?
3) _____ ?
4) _____ ?
5) _____
6) _____

J+

WELL, MAYBE YOU COULD REMIND MISS HOOVER OF WHY SHE GOT INTO TEACHING. TAKE HER TO SOME INSPIRING EDUCATIONAL PLACES.

HMM... OKAY. THANKS, MOM.

SURE. NOW IN THE MEAN TIME...

...COULD YOU GRAB THE TOASTER AND PULL?

DAD, ARE YOU STILL HOLDING ON TO YOUR TOAST?

MAYBE.

THE NEXT DAY...

TEACHERS' LOUNGE

POOR MISS HOOVER. SHE MUST BE GOING THROUGH A MID-LIFE CRISIS. I HOPE I CAN REACH HER BEFORE SHE HITS ROCK BOTTOM.

The Secret Garden

OH, MY GOSH! IT'S WORSE THAN I THOUGHT!

♫ WELL, I GOT ♫ FRIENDS IN LOOOOW ♪ PLACES... ♪

MISS HOOVER, PULL YOURSELF TOGETHER! YOU CAN'T LET YOUR COLLEAGUES *SEE* YOU LIKE THIS!

WHO CARES? MOST OF 'EM ARE MORE MISERABLE THAN ME! IT'S TIME I LET YOU IN ON A LITTLE SECRET, LISA. YOU KNOW THAT OLD SAYING, "THOSE WHO CAN, *DO* AND THOSE WHO CAN'T, *TEACH*"?

YES.

IT'S *TRUE!* ALL TEACHERS ARE FAILURES! MRS. KRABAPPEL WANTED TO BE A DANCER. PRINCIPAL SKINNER WANTED TO BE A SCIENTIST. AND MR. LARGO, YOUR BAND TEACHER--

WANTED TO BE A GREAT MUSICIAN?

YOU'D THINK SO, BUT NO. HE WANTED TO BE THE IRON CHEF. EVERY TIME HE SEES A WHISK, HE STARTS BAWLING LIKE A BABY.

OH, THAT'S SAD. AND WHAT DID *YOU* WANT TO BE?

THAT'S THE IRONIC PART! I REALLY WANTED TO BE A TEACHER. BUT I FAILED YOU, FAILED THE OTHER KIDS...THE ONLY THING LEFT FOR ME IS TO BECOME A DRUNK AND REPLACE GROUNDSKEEPER WILLIE AFTER HE DIES.

NO! YOU'RE BETTER THAN THAT! TEACHING IS THE NOBLEST PROFESSION THERE IS. LET ME HELP YOU REMEMBER WHY YOU STARTED.

BUT WHO WILL TEACH YOUR CLASS?

SURE. WHY NOT? LET'S GET OUT OF HERE. THIS PLACE IS DEPRESSING.

SNACKS

RALPH ALREADY GRADED THE TESTS, SO...

"...HOW MUCH DAMAGE CAN HE DO BABYSITTING THE CLASS FOR ONE DAY?"

I CAN SPIN IN CIRCLES UNTIL MY TUMMY GOES WHOOPSIE!

SOON...

LOOK, MISS HOOVER, IT'S A STEGOSAURUS. I'LL BET YOU KNOW LOTS OF AMAZING FACTS ABOUT IT.

NOT REALLY. DINOSAURS WERE LIKE GIANT, GREEN, STUPID CATS. AND I'M GLAD I DIDN'T HAVE TO CLEAN *THAT* LITTER BOX.

STEGOSAURUS

UM...OKAY...WHAT ABOUT THE EGYPTIAN WING? THE ANCIENT EGYPTIANS WERE PRETTY ADVANCED FOR THEIR TIME. I'LL BET THERE ARE ALL SORTS OF THINGS I DON'T KNOW ABOUT THEM.

LISA, YOUR AVERAGE ABBOTT AND COSTELLO MOVIE HAS EVERYTHING YOU'LL EVER NEED TO KNOW ABOUT MUMMIES. AND IF THE ANCIENT EGYPTIANS WERE SO SMART, WHY ARE THEY ALL DEAD?

EGYPTIAN WING

NEFERTITI

OKAY, THIS IS DEFINITELY ONE YOU'LL BE IMPRESSED WITH. JOHN ADAMS WAS A *FOUNDING FATHER* OF OUR COUNTRY, THE *SECOND PRESIDENT* OF THE UNITED STATES, THE *FATHER* OF A PRESIDENT, AND A *TEACHER*. SEE...THEY'RE NOT *ALL* FAILURES.

WELL...

JOHN ADAMS

IF HE WAS SUCH A SUCCESS, WHY WASN'T HE THE *FIRST* PRESIDENT? WHERE'S *HIS* DOLLAR BILL?

D'OH! FORGET IT. WHY DON'T WE TRY THE JAZZ CLUB.

NOW THIS IS A REAL CULTURAL SCENE. JAZZ MUSIC, THE COMPANY OF INTELLECTUALS, AND INTERNATIONAL COFFEES.

MEH.

OH, WHAT IS IT *NOW*?

WELL, I DIDN'T WANT TO SAY ANY-THING, BUT THIS INTER-NATIONAL COFFEE IS FROM *CANADA*. THAT'S LIKE *AMERICA-LITE*. NOT VERY EXOTIC.

ONTARIO'S INTERNATIONAL COFFEE WE'RE ALL ABOOT THE FLAVOR!

FACE IT, LISA, THE PASSION I HAD FOR TEACHING IS AS GONE AS THE PASSION THE GOP ONCE HAD FOR LIMITED GOVERNMENT.

PASSION, HMM? I'VE BEEN GOING ABOUT THIS ALL WRONG. IF IT'S *PASSION* SHE WANTS, THEN IT'S PASSION SHE *GETS!*

THE NEXT DAY...

SO YOU LOST YOUR WILL TO TEACH, HUH?

YEAH.

WELCOME TO THE CLUB.

THINK IT'S TOO LATE FOR US TO BECOME MOB MISTRESSES?

PROBABLY.

MISS HOOVER...

...THIS IS UMBERTO. HE'S A POOL BOY.

I LIKE-A THE TEACHERS. THEY'RE GOOD AT OILING UP-A MY RIPPLING MUSCLES. MAYBE WE CAN GO SOMEWHERE AND YOU TELL-A ME ALL YOUR TROUBLES, HUH?

LISA, WHERE DID YOU FIND THIS...THIS...

GOD AMONG MEN!

HE WAS IN OUR NEIGHBOR MR. FLANDERS' BIBLE STUDY GROUP.

I LIKE-A THE MARRIAGE. SOME DAY I HOPE TO HAVE-A MANY CHILDREN.

PASS.

WHAT?!

I NO UNDERSTAND.

UMBERTO IS PERFECT! WHAT COULD POSSIBLY BE WRONG WITH HIM?!

IT'LL NEVER WORK OUT. I DON'T EVEN HAVE A POOL. BESIDES, HE LOOKS TO BE MORE EDNA'S SPEED.

C'MON, HANDSOME. I'VE GOT A LITTLE POOL YOU CAN CLEAN. IT'S CALLED MY BATH TUB! HA!

I DON'T BELIEVE THIS...

YOU KNOW WHAT YOUR PROBLEM IS?! YOU DON'T *WANT* TO BE HAPPY! YOUR MISERY IS THE ONLY THING YOU KNOW... SO IT'S *COMFORTING*!

LISA!

IT'S *TRUE!* YOU'RE NOT JUST MISERABLE ABOUT TEACHING, YOU'RE MISERABLE ABOUT YOUR WHOLE *LIFE!* AND RATHER THAN TRYING TO BE HAPPY, YOU JUST MAKE EVERYONE ELSE *CRAZY!*

WAIT A MINUTE. *LISA!* I THINK YOU *HAVE* IT!

YOU'RE RIGHT! I *DON'T* LIKE TO TEACH! BUT I *DO* LIKE TO *FRUSTRATE* MY STUDENTS BY MESSING WITH THEM!

WHAT?!

I'VE GOT TO GET BACK TO MY CLASS AND DO WHAT I WAS *BORN* TO DO!

CLASS, LET'S BEGIN BY REWRITING CHAPTER ONE OF YOUR LANGUAGE ARTS TEXT IN YOUR NOTEBOOKS.

BUT REWRITING THE CHAPTER WON'T TEACH US *ANYTHING!*

THAT'S *RIGHT!* THANK YOU, LISA...FOR EVERYTHING.

BUT... BUT...

QUIET, LISA! I'M TRYING TO BE LEARN-DED.

I'VE GOT LOTS OF BUSY WORK FOR YOU ALL TODAY!

UGH... WHAT HAVE I DONE...?

THE END

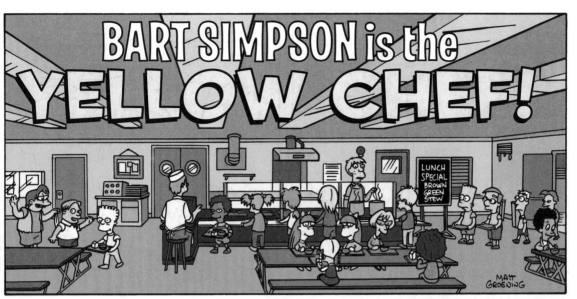

BART SIMPSON is the YELLOW CHEF!

NEITHER OF THESE LOOK VERY *SPECIAL* TO ME.

LUNCH SPECIAL

WHAT'S THE DIFFERENCE BETWEEN THE BROWN STEW AND THE GREEN STEW?

WELL...ONE IS BROWN AND THE OTHER IS GREEN.

JAMES W. BATES
SCRIPT

MARCOS ASPREC
PENCILS

SHANE GLINES
INKS

NATHAN HAMILL
COLORS

KAREN BATES
LETTERS

BILL MORRISON
EDITOR

GREAT GOOGLY MOOGLY! GIL, **YOU'RE** THE CHEF IN THIS KITCHEN NIGHTMARE?

I JUST GOT THE JOB.

YOUR FOOD HAS GOT ME IN A BAD MOOD.

WHAT DID YOU EXPECT TO FIND BACK HERE? A GOURMET, FIVE-STAR KITCHEN?

I DID HOPE TO FIND SOME GRUB THAT DOESN'T SMELL LIKE OLD SNEAKERS.

YOU GOTTA UNDERSTAND...I CAN ONLY COOK WITH WHAT THE SCHOOL DISTRICT GIVES ME.

PLEASE DON'T COMPLAIN ABOUT 'OL GIL. IF I LOSE **ONE MORE** JOB, I'LL HAVE TO SELL **ANOTHER** ORGAN.

LOOK AT ALL THESE SPICES! WHAT THIS KITCHEN NEEDS IS A LITTLE BART SIMPSON *SAVOIR FAIRE*.

WHENEVER KRUSTY IS AIRING RE-RUNS, I WATCH THAT *ANGRY CHEF* SHOW. I'VE GOT SOME IDEAS.

IDEAS?

GREAT IDEAS! LET'S GET COOKING!

WE'RE NOT JUST GONNA MAKE LUNCH. WE'RE GONNA *MAKE HISTORY!*

I NEED *SALISBURY STEAK!*

YES, CHEF!

I NEED *FISH STICKS!*

YES, CHEF!

I NEED *TATER TOTS!*

YES, CHEF!!!

I'LL LET THE *SALISBURY STEAK SKEWERS* MARINATE IN TERIYAKI SAUCE AND THEN SPRINKLE THEM WITH SESAME SEEDS AFTER GRILLING.

THE *MACARONI AND FROMAGE TATER TOT CASSEROLE* IS LOOKING GOOD!

I KNEW IT WOULD BE BETTER IF WE ADDED *CHEESE* INSTEAD OF *CHEEZ!*

CHEF, WHAT DO YOU THINK OF MY DARTH VADER FISH STICK FUNERAL PYRE?

THOSE ARE DANCING EWOKS.

THE FORCE IS DEFINITELY WITH YOU! THE BURNT FISH STICK IS VADER, BUT WHAT'S WITH THE TATER TOTS?

BUT WILL THE DINERS LIKE BART'S CULINARY CREATIONS?

MMM!!!

CHECK IT OUT! WENDELL'S ACTUALLY KEEPING HIS LUNCH DOWN!

FOR ONCE I DON'T WANT TO SMASH MY LUNCH OVER THE CLOSEST NERD'S HEAD!

HUZZAH!

MMM. I HAVE TO ADMIT THE TERIYAKI SAUCE HIDES THE USUAL AFTERTASTE.

I CAN HARDLY TELL THAT IT'S A LOW-GRADE BEEF SUBSTITUTE.

DID WE REALLY MAKE SOMETHING GOOD?

LET'S ASK *THEM!*

WHAT DO YOU THINK? IS THIS *THE BEST SCHOOL LUNCH EVER?*

BART SIMPSON in SPLIT DECISIONS

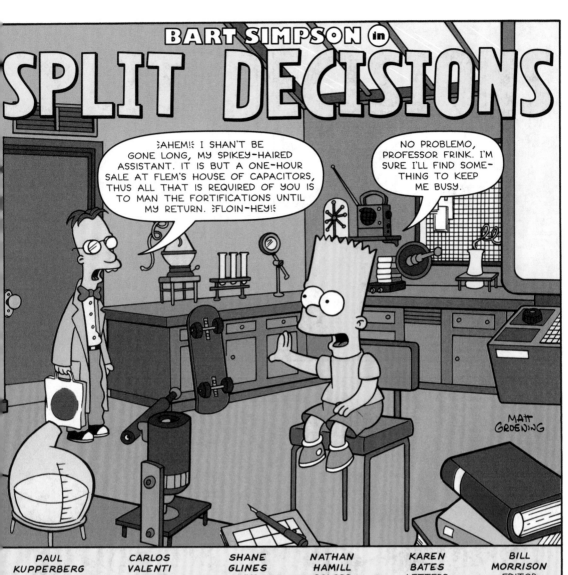

:AHEM!: I SHAN'T BE GONE LONG, MY SPIKEY-HAIRED ASSISTANT. IT IS BUT A ONE-HOUR SALE AT FLEM'S HOUSE OF CAPACITORS, THUS ALL THAT IS REQUIRED OF YOU IS TO MAN THE FORTIFICATIONS UNTIL MY RETURN. :FLOIN-HEY!:

NO PROBLEMO, PROFESSOR FRINK. I'M SURE I'LL FIND SOMETHING TO KEEP ME BUSY.

MATT GROENING

PAUL KUPPERBERG	CARLOS VALENTI	SHANE GLINES	NATHAN HAMILL	KAREN BATES	BILL MORRISON
SCRIPT	PENCILS	INKS	COLORS	LETTERS	EDITOR

TOUCH *NOTHING*, BART! NEED I REMIND YOU THAT THIS ROOM HOUSES FORCES WITH WHICH MERE MORTALS SHOULD *FEAR* TO MEDDLE?!

GEEZ, MAN. BREAK JUST *ONE* NUCLEAR CONTAINMENT UNIT, AND YOU *NEVER* HEAR THE END OF IT!

A WORD TO THE *WISE*, MY BOY. :WOO-*HOY*!:

SLAM!

HEH! GOOD ADVICE...*IF* ANYBODY WAS LISTENING, NERDZILLA!

MAN, HOW BORING IS THIS? OL' FRINKENSTEIN NEEDS TO GET A GAMESTER 3000 OR...*WHOA!*

OH, MAMA! WHERE HAVE YOU BEEN ALL MY LIFE?

PLEASE HAVE A *CABLE* HOOK-UP...

...AND BE ABLE TO GET "ITCHY & SCRATCHY UNPLUGGED" ON PAY-PER-VIEW!

KLIK!

HUH?

NOT ONLY IS THIS BORING, IT'S PATHETIC.

FRINK, OL' PAL, YOU'RE THE WORST PEEPING TOM *EVER!*

KLIK! KLIK! KLIK! KLIK!

WHOA!

FZZZZAP!

THUD!

BUMP!

BUMP!

HA HA HA! AGAIN!

WHICH BUTTON DID I PUSH TO ...WHA--?! THAT'S ME ON THE SCREEN...

...AND... ANOTHER ME? SAY, WHAT KIND OF A SCREWY SET-UP IS THIS?

YEAH, MAN, I DECIDED THAT THING'S TOO DANGEROUS TO TOUCH!

AYE, CARUMBA! I'VE BEEN CLONED!

I DON'T THINK SO, MAN. THIS THING SAYS IT'S A MULTI-DIMENSIONAL... SOMETHING...SOME-THING...VIEWER.

MULTI-DIMENSIONAL TRANSEXPONENTIAL FENESTRATION VIEWER

SO, IN THEORY, I COULD SEE SOME BIG, FAT *TARGET* UP AHEAD...

...AND DO THE COMPLETELY *RIGHT* THING BY PASSING HIM BY...

HIYA, MOE!

YOUR YOUTHFUL ENTHUSIASM MAKES ME SICK, PUNK!

OW!

HEH HEH!

...BUT STILL GET COMPLETE *ALTERNATE-SELF-SATISFACTION* BY TAKING HIM DOWN!

WHEN I GET MY HANDS ON *YOU*...

...I'LL *STRANGLE* YOU!

...I'LL DUCT TAPE YOUR MOUTH TO THE EXHAUST PIPE OF MY *YUGO*!

OH BOY, I'M *CONTAGIOUS*! IT WORKS ON OTHER PEOPLE, TOO!

THE ANDROID'S DUNGEON & BASEBALL CARD SHOP

HEY, COMIC BOOK GUY! I GOT A QUESTION FOR YOU...

WHATEVER IT IS, SIMPSON, THE ANSWER IS AN EMPHATIC *NO*!

CALM DOWN, MAN! I WAS JUST WONDERING, IN YOUR EXPERT OPINION, WHICH OF THE ALTERNATE-EARTHS SHOULD BE SAVED IN MEGASTORM COMICS' "ULTIMATE COSMIC CRISIS IN TIME"?

HMM...YOU POSE AN INTRIGUING QUESTION, AT THAT...

120

WAIT 'TIL HOMER SEES THIS!

HEY, HOMIE! GET A LOAD OF THIS...!

HA! I SHOULD'VE OFFERED HIM A CHOICE BETWEEN DONUTS AND PORK RINDS.

OOOOOH! WHAT SHOULD I DO FIRST...?!

SLAMM!

HOW COME THERE'S STILL ONLY ONE OF YOU, FLANDERS?

YEAH, EVERY TIME ONE OF US MAKES A CHOICE THERE ARE MORE OF US...EXCEPT FOR YOU!

WELL, GOSH-A-ROONIE, GUYS, I LEAVE THE DECISIONS UP TO THE GREAT DECIDER IN THE SKY. I HAVEN'T MADE A CHOICE IN YEARS.

MATH ISN'T EXACTLY MY *BEST* SUBJECT...

...BUT IF *EVERY* NEW ME SPLITS INTO *MORE* ME'S WITH EVERY DECISION...

...AND THEN *THOSE* ME'S ALSO SPLIT...

...AND SO ON AND SO FORTH...

...UHM, CARRY THE THREE, DIVIDED BY SEVEN...

...PRETTY SOON, EVERYBODY'S GOING TO DECIDE THEY WANNA KILL ME, CREATING DECISION-DUPLICATES THAT'LL DECIDE TO DO JUST *THAT!*

AYE, CARUMBA!

THERE I AM! GET ME!

HUH?

DID SOMEONE SAY DONUTS?

AND PORK RINDS?

YOU GET THEM.

NO, YOU.

I WAS HERE FIRST.

I THOUGHT WE WERE GONNA BE FRIENDS.

I GOTTA GET BACK TO FRINK'S PLACE! ALL THIS STARTED WHEN I WAS PLAYING AROUND WITH THAT MACHINE.

MAYBE IF I TURN IT OFF...?

NO, WE NEED TO KNOCK OUT THE POWER GRID FOR THE ENTIRE CITY!

DON'T LOOK AT ME, DUDE....*YOU* THOUGHT IT!

WHA--?! THAT'S NOT GONNA HELP!

125

THE END

BART DRAWS A STRIP

THIS IS LISA.

She likes to smell stinky FLOWERS!

I am a total GIRL... Yuck!

She likes to read stinky BOOKS!

DUH! I'M A REAL BRAINIAC!

How to BE DUMB!

Suddenly a ferocious ~~RINO RYNO~~ TIGER attacks!!

!!

Go, tiger, go!!! You can do it!!!

EEEEK!

ROAR! ROAR!

Lisa finds a cave to hide in. Too bad!! Poor tiger!!!

I will hide!

Lucky for us, there's another TIGER in that cave! Ha! Ha! Ha!

ROAR! BITE! SNARL! GRR!!!! CHEW!!

AAAA! He's eating me up! Ow!

ALL YOUR COMIC STRIPS ARE ABOUT ME BEING EATEN BY ANIMALS!

YOU WOULDN'T *BELIEVE* HOW MUCH I SPEND ON *RED CRAYONS!*

MATT GROENING